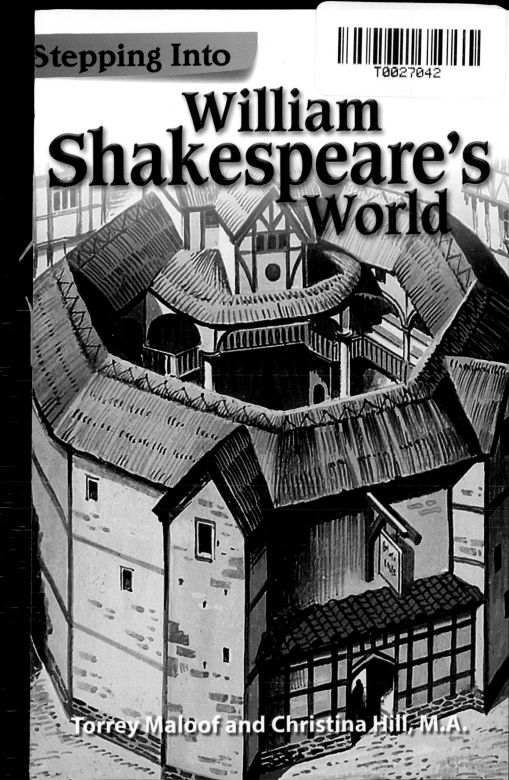

Stepping Into

William
Shakespeare's
World

Torrey Maloof and Christina Hill, M.A.

T0027042

Consultants

Timothy Rasinski, Ph.D.
Kent State University

Lori Oczkus, M.A.
Literacy Consultant

Publishing Credits

Rachelle Cracchiolo, M.S.Ed., *Publisher*

Conni Medina, M.A.Ed., *Managing Editor*

Dona Herweck Rice, *Series Developer*

Emily R. Smith, M.A.Ed., *Content Director*

Stephanie Bernard/Susan Daddis, M.A.Ed., *Editors*

Robin Erickson, *Senior Graphic Designer*

The TIME logo is a registered trademark of TIME Inc. Used under license.

Image Credits: p.2 Funny Solution Studio/Shutterstock.com; p.4 Felipe Trueba/Alamy Stock Photo; p.6 Ken Welsh/Alamy Stock Photo; pp.6–7 iStock.com/claudiodivizia; pp.8–9 Wellcome Library, London, used under CC BY 4.0; p.9 Old Paper Studios/Alamy Stock Photo; pp.12–13 Dorling Kindersley/Getty Images; p.13 Folger Shakespeare Library; p.14 FromOldBooks.org/Alamy Stock Photo; p.17 Mary Evans Picture Library/Alamy Stock Photo; p.21 Encyclopedia Britannica; pp.22–23 akg-images/Newscom; pp.24–25 Bettman/Getty Images; pp.30–31 SOTK2011/Alamy Stock Photo; p.33 Rijksmuseum, Amsterdam, The Netherlands; p.41 Timothy J. Bradley; p.43 (top left) GL Archive/Alamy Stock Photo; p.43 (top right) Wikimedia Commons/Public Domain; p.43 (back) Wikimedia Commons/Public Domain; all other images from iStock and/or Shutterstock.

Library of Congress Cataloging-in-Publication Data

Names: Maloof, Torrey, author. | Hill, Christina, author.
Title: The world of William Shakespeare / Torrey Maloof and Christina Hill.
Description: Huntington Beach, CA : Teacher Created Materials, 2017. | Includes index.
Identifiers: LCCN 2016026806 (print) | LCCN 2016043438 (ebook) | ISBN 9781493836185 (pbk.) | ISBN 9781480757226 (eBook)
Subjects: LCSH: Shakespeare, William, 1564-1616--Juvenile literature. | Dramatists, English--Early modern, 1500-1700--Biography--Juvenile literature. | England--Civilization--16th century--Juvenile literature.
Classification: LCC PR2895 .M35 2017 (print) | LCC PR2895 (ebook) | DDC 822.3/3 [B] --dc23
LC record available at https://lccn.loc.gov/2016026806

Teacher Created Materials

5301 Oceanus Drive
Huntington Beach, CA 92649-1030
http://www.tcmpub.com

ISBN 978-1-4938-3618-5

© 2017 Teacher Created Materials, Inc.
Printed in China
Nordica.082019.CA21901021

Table of Contents

Will's World

Would you pay $6.2 million for a book? In the year 2001, someone did! The book purchased was a copy of William Shakespeare's *First Folio*. There are believed to be only 230 copies of the *First Folio* in the world. It is a prized possession sought by many book collectors. But what makes this book so special and expensive? This folio was the first collected edition of Shakespeare's plays.

It was published in 1623, seven years after he died. Without it, 18 of his plays may not have been recorded.

First Folio, Where Art Thou?

A census is the official process of counting the number of people in a country, city, or town. But there is also a census for the *First Folio*! Scholars are working to track down the estimated 230 copies and possibly find more.

The Bard, as he is sometimes called, is one of the most popular and well-known authors in the world. Many people consider him to be the greatest playwright of all time. His poems and plays are masterpieces of human emotion and **psychology**. His skillful use of language, his unforgettable characters, and his unique ability to relate stories have helped Shakespeare's work stand the test of time.

Shakespeare lived and wrote during the Tudor period in England, which was mainly in the sixteenth century. The Tudors were an English royal dynasty that ruled from 1485 to 1603. As you can imagine, life was quite different then. By stepping into Shakespeare's world, we can gain a better understanding and appreciation of his works, and we can learn why, almost 500 years later, his works still appeal to the masses.

First Folio Facts

The *First Folio* contains 36 of Shakespeare's plays and is more than 900 pages long! It also includes one of only two portraits proven to be William Shakespeare.

Getting to Know the Bard

Just who was William Shakespeare? Despite his popularity, people today do not know a lot about him. Back then, records were rarely kept on average individuals. Shakespeare's exact date of birth is not known. However, historians believe he was born on April 23, 1564, to John and Mary Shakespeare in the small market town of Stratford, England. What we do know is that he was **baptized** on April 26. He was the third of eight children and the firstborn son of the family. His father was a successful businessman who made and sold gloves. Later, he became a member of the town council. John was a well-respected man and made important decisions for the town.

Shakespeare most likely attended a local school in Stratford. Unfortunately, after his baptism, Shakespeare's name is not mentioned again in any official records until 1582. That year, at age 18, he married a woman named Anne Hathaway, who was about 26 years old. The couple had three children. They had a daughter named Susanna and twins, Hamnet and Judith. The young family most likely lived with Shakespeare's parents.

baptismal record of William Shakespeare

Decline in Status

Later in life, John Shakespeare became absent from town council records. Some people believe it was because he lost his money. Others believe it was because of religious disputes.

Shakespeare's Home

If you ever travel to England, be sure to visit Stratford, also known as Stratford-upon-Avon. You can take a tour of the house in which Shakespeare was born and raised. Many famous authors have visited the house over the years, including Charles Dickens and John Keats.

Shakespeare in London

Shortly after his twins were born, Shakespeare left Stratford for unknown reasons. By 1592, he was an actor and a playwright living in the bustling city of London. It is not clear exactly how this happened, but we do know that by age 28, he was successful—*very* successful!

Shakespeare's plays were extremely popular in London. He made his money by selling his plays to acting **troupes** and by performing in them in theaters. He was doing very well for himself until the **plague** hit London.

Poetry and the Plague

From 1592 to 1594, the plague ravaged London. This was a terrifying and deadly disease caused by bacteria. It traveled from person to person at an alarming rate. Hundreds of thousands of people died. The theaters closed in an attempt to stop the spread of the deadly disease. Many of the theater troupes **disbanded** and left the city. Shakespeare most likely left London, too. During this dark time, Shakespeare turned his attention to writing poetry. A **patron** supported him, and a publisher purchased some of his poems and all 154 of his **sonnets**.

The Lost Years

From 1585 to 1592, Shakespeare is missing from all records. Historians know he left Stratford, but they do not know why or where he went. Scholars call this period his "lost years." There are many different theories about how he spent his time. Some people believe he joined a traveling theater troupe.

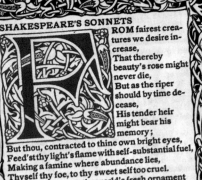

SHAKESPEARE'S SONNETS

FROM fairest creatures we desire increase,
That thereby beauty's rose might never die,
But as the riper should by time decease,
His tender heir might bear his memory;
But thou, contracted to thine own bright eyes,
Feed'st thy light's flame with self-substantial fuel,
Making a famine where abundance lies,
Thyself thy foe, to thy sweet self too cruel.
Thou, that art now the world's fresh ornament
And only herald to the gaudy spring,
Within thine own bud buriest thy content
And, tender churl, mak'st waste in niggarding.
Pity the world, or else this glutton be,
To eat the world's due, by the grave and thee.

Shakespeare's Sonnets

A sonnet is a poem with exactly 14 lines and a fixed rhyme scheme. Shakespeare's 154 sonnets are heavy with metaphors. Most of them primarily focus on the universal topic of love.

The Plague in Shakespeare's Day

The plague killed about 25 million people across Europe during its reign of terror. Here are some interesting—and disturbing—facts about the plague's attacks on Elizabethan London.

Symptom Checker

How did you know if you had the plague in Shakespeare's day? You would look for these symptoms.

- swollen **lymph nodes** (the size of chicken eggs) in your armpits, groin, or neck
- sudden and severe fever with chills
- pounding headache
- vomiting
- coughing up blood
- bleeding under the skin
- uncontrollable muscle spasms

Aw, Rats!

If you saw a rat during a plague outbreak, it would be a good idea to RUN AWAY! Fleas on rats carried the disease. When a rat died, the fleas would look for other hosts.

Escaping the Plague

Back then, people did not know what caused the plague. Here are some things they would do to try to avoid catching it.

- wear special charms
- confess and apologize to God for any sins
- carry fragrant flowers in their pockets
- carry **pomanders**

pomander

Elizabethan Outbreaks

There were multiple outbreaks of the plague during Shakespeare's time. This chart shows the most severe outbreaks in London.

Year	Population before	Population after
1563	85,000	67,596
1593	125,000	114,325
1603	141,000	115,955

plague doctor

A Theater of His Own

After the threat of the plague passed, Shakespeare returned to London and theater life. He became part owner of a theater troupe called the Lord Chamberlain's Men. He wrote some of his most famous plays during this time, including *Romeo and Juliet* and *A Midsummer Night's Dream*.

In 1599, Shakespeare and his troupe built a new theater called the Globe. *Julius Caesar* was one of the first plays performed there. After Queen Elizabeth I died in 1603, the Lord Chamberlain's Men continued producing plays. They became known as the King's Men under King James I. This was a huge honor, and the troupe quickly became the most famous group of actors in all of England.

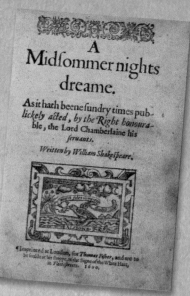

All's Well That Ends Well

Shakespeare continued to write very successful plays. Between 1610 and 1613, it appears that he may have quit acting and returned to his hometown of Stratford. He died on April 23, 1616, at the age of 52.

While we may not know much about the biographical details of Shakespeare's life, we do know a lot about the time in which he lived. This information helps us learn more about Shakespeare and also provides insight into his life's work.

Other Options

Theater was not the only form of entertainment in Shakespeare's day. Watching public executions was quite popular. There were gallows to hang traitors and guillotines to cut off heads. Large crowds would gather to watch these gruesome and gory death scenes.

The High and the Low

Social classes were divided in the Tudor period, with the highest rank being, of course, the **monarch**. During Shakespeare's time, Queen Elizabeth I ruled, followed by King James I. Most people remained within the social class in which they were born. However, a few motivated citizens managed to climb the social ladder. Shakespeare was certainly one of those ambitious citizens!

A Play about Social Mobility

The changing roles of the merchant class are depicted in Shakespeare's play *The Merchant of Venice*. This play gives insight into class struggles and prejudices of the time. It also explores a person's ability to use wealth to achieve a higher social status and to gain power.

clothing of the nobles and wealthy

Nobility and Gentry

The highest social class was the rich and powerful landowners, born into noble families. There were about 55 noble families in England during Shakespeare's time.

The **gentry** were wealthy like the nobility but lacked noble titles. Nevertheless, they were well educated and respected. Most of them did not have actual jobs, with the exception of knights and **squires**. The gentry received income by collecting rent on the properties they owned.

Merchants and Yeomanry

During the Tudor era, the merchant class grew. This is because merchants became wealthy through trade.

The **yeomanry** was often called the "middling" class. They owned land and worked at skilled crafts or trades. While this was one of the lower social classes, most of the members attended some form of school and were mostly literate. Shakespeare was born into this class.

Unifying the Classes

Despite the division of social classes, one thing united the people of London—love of the theater! Members from every class enjoyed attending plays. Most people paid a penny to stand in the yard to watch, while wealthier citizens paid more to sit in seats.

Laborers and the Poor

The lowest social class was made up of the poor peasants in England who did not own land. Some peasants had jobs as masons, shoemakers, or day laborers. Others were beggars. Most people in this class were **illiterate** and never attended school. Queen Elizabeth I issued the English Poor Laws to raise money to help these citizens. Still, life was bleak and difficult for those at the bottom of the social system.

Social Mobility

It was challenging to move upward on the social-class ladder. Yet, Shakespeare was determined to prove himself worthy of being called a gentleman. In 1596, Shakespeare applied for a coat of arms, which is a group of symbols shown on a shield that represents a person or a family. He filled out the application in his father's name. The request was granted, and Shakespeare's family was then considered gentry. After this time, Shakespeare requested to be called "Master Shakespeare" and signed some of his legal documents with his name, followed by *gent*, which stood for "gentleman."

English folk art

STOP! THINK...

Analyze the image of Shakespeare's coat of arms to answer the questions:

- ◉ What elements are part of the design? What significance do you think they have to Shakespeare's family name?

- ◉ The motto reads "*Non Sanz Droict*," which translates to "Not Without Right." What do you think this means?

- ◉ Why do you think purchasing the coat of arms for his family was so important to Shakespeare?

NON SANZ DROICT.

The Arms of Shakspere

London Printed for J.Bell British Library Strand Jan 3.1787.

Merely a Player

In 1602, a complaint was filed for issuing coats of arms to unworthy people. Shakespeare was listed as one person who was undeserving because of his profession as a player, or actor. Ultimately, the claim was dismissed.

Symbols

There are more than a thousand references to the Bible in Shakespeare's writing. Shakespeare also drew heavily upon the supernatural realm. His plays are filled with ghosts, angels, witches, wizards, magic, and enchanting spells.

Beliefs

Religion was closely tied to politics during this time. Citizens were forced to follow the religion of the current monarch. For years, England was torn between the Anglican Church (also known as Protestants) and the Catholic Church.

From 1553 to 1558, Queen Mary ruled. She required her subjects to be Catholic. When Queen Elizabeth I took the throne in 1558, she returned England to the Anglican Church. Citizens were forced to convert. They were required to attend church, and if they didn't, they faced **persecution**.

Divine Right

At that time, people believed that God **ordained** the royal family to rule. The divine right gave the monarchy absolute power that was subject only to God's will. That is why the monarch acted as both head of the country and head of the church. There was no separation between religion and political power.

Catholic or Protestant?

Little is known about Shakespeare's religious beliefs. Some historians speculate that Shakespeare's father remained Catholic, even under Protestant rule. We know that John stopped going to religious council meetings. Some experts think he was practicing Catholic traditions in secret at home.

Shakespeare's religious preference remains a topic of debate. However, it is certain that religion was part of his life. This is reflected in his writing. All of Shakespeare's plays are full of biblical **allusions** that both Protestants and Catholics would understand.

Religious Influence on the Theater

Many people looked down on the theater, including leaders of the Anglican Church. Religious officials believed actors had questionable **morals**. Acting was not considered a proper or respectable profession. Plays often contained language and themes that were considered vulgar or rude. The Church leaders also feared that people would choose to attend plays over going to church.

Queen Elizabeth I enjoyed the theater immensely. So, she set up rules to protect both playwrights and the Anglican Church. These rules helped keep theater alive. First, each play had to be reviewed and approved by the Master of Revels before it could be performed. This gave the government the power to **censor** any play. Plays that spoke negatively about the Church or the monarchy were censored. To please the Church, plays were discouraged from being performed on Sundays or other holy days.

London Theatres c. 1600

Just Around the Corner!

Queen Elizabeth I allowed public playhouses, or theaters, to be built as long as they were not within London's city borders. This made it easy for the people from the city to attend theater productions.

Master of Revels

Edmund Tilney was the Master of Revels under the reign of Queen Elizabeth I. Initially, the job description was to plan parties and keep the queen entertained. However, Tilney took over the role of censor. No play could be performed without his stamp of approval.

Education

In Shakespeare's day, it was not **mandatory** for children to go to school. Although both boys and girls could attend school in Tudor England, it was mainly boys who went. Poor children were less likely to go to school because they could not afford it and their help was needed at home. The upper classes and nobility would often hire private tutors to teach their children rather than send them to school.

Young children (usually around five years old) attended petty schools to learn to read. After petty schools, children could attend grammar schools until age 16. Grammar school days would often start at sunrise and end near sunset. Children attended school six days a week all year long, only getting Sundays and a few holidays off. Perhaps, this rigid and draining schedule is why Shakespeare mentions a "whining schoolboy" who was "creeping like a snail unwillingly to school" in his play *As You Like It*.

Education for Girls

Girls sometimes attended petty school to learn how to read; however, they rarely continued to grammar school. Most girls were educated at home by their mothers and were taught household duties, music, and dance. The few girls who were taught more were usually from very rich or noble families.

Better Behave

If children misbehaved in school, they would be disciplined physically. Some teachers would tie a handful of birch sticks together and hit the children.

King Edward VI Grammar School in Stratford-upon-Avon, assumed school of William Shakespeare

Topics Taught

Reading was considered an important skill during this time period because it allowed a person to study and interpret the Bible. The ability to read was also useful in business matters. Students were typically taught to read using hornbooks. These were wooden paddles that contained the alphabet and words from the Lord's Prayer. Writing was also taught using paper and **quills**. Students learned rhetoric, too. This is the art of learning how to speak and write formally to persuade people. Students would learn history, philosophy, and literature in their later years in school.

After Grammar School

Men from the upper class could attend universities. With university degrees, they could teach, become lawyers, practice medicine, or have careers in the Church. Other men learned trades as apprentices, such as tailors, blacksmiths, or cooks.

quill and ink

All About Latin

Latin was a crucial part of school as it was the language of educated people and the Church. Students learned to read and write in Latin. By age 10, many students were reciting speeches and reading books in this classical language. As adults, church services and laws were written in Latin, so it was beneficial to know this ancient language.

The A.B.C

Set foꝛthe by the Kynges maiestie and his Clergye, and commaunded to be taught thꝛough out all his Realme. All other bokes set apart, as the teachers thereof tendꝛe his graces fauour.

a b c d e f g h i k l m, n o p q r ſ s t u v w x, y z ꝯ z: Eſt. Amen.

a hornbook

Learned Man

Shakespeare did not attend a university. Yet he demonstrated a great wealth of knowledge in his work. This suggests that he did receive some type of education. Many experts think he must have had natural genius as well.

Daily Life

Life in Elizabethan England was far different from life today. Homes had no electricity or running water. Entertainment was found in books, music, and theater instead of on televisions, computers, and smart phones. The main mode of transportation for most people was walking. The comforts and luxuries of our modern world were nonexistent!

Still, some things have remained the same. People enjoyed parties and social events, and they gathered together for mealtimes. And, just like today, fashion was important to many people. Exaggerated clothing was all the rage!

Sumptuary Statutes

Queen Elizabeth I issued the Sumptuary Statutes, which were laws restricting extravagance in clothing. The goal was to divide social classes; however, the laws were impossible to enforce. Over time, the lower classes wore clothing styles similar to those of the nobility but with fewer jewels and made with cheaper fabric.

THINK LINK

◉ Why might people have wanted their attire to resemble that of Queen Elizabeth I?

◉ For what reasons would Queen Elizabeth I have cared so much about what her citizens wore?

◉ Why did the government set restrictions on fashion?

What to Wear

Today, we look to fashion designers for the latest trends. But in Shakespeare's world, the monarch determined fashion styles. Queen Elizabeth I was known for her extravagant dresses. As the years passed, her costumes became more extreme. She set fashion trends that filtered into all levels of society. Even men's fashion changed to follow these new styles.

Queen Elizabeth I also issued restrictions on clothing. For instance, she demanded that members of the royal family were the only people who could wear purple clothing. Her subjects willingly followed this regulation because no one could afford purple dye.

Male Fashion

During Shakespeare's time, fashion styles for men moved away from the traditional style of long tunic dresses that were worn during the reign of Henry VIII. These tunics were replaced with tight-fitting jackets called doublets. Eventually, men began wearing padding underneath the jackets, which gave them large, rounded waistlines. The most memorable item from this period may be the ruff. It was a large ruffled collar that flared out around the neck. Men also wore breeches, which looked like pairs of inflated, puffy shorts. They finished their looks with stockings and boots. In addition, hats of all kinds were very fashionable.

Starch Saves the Ruff

People wanted their ruffs to be large and extend far and wide around their necks. The only problem was that the fabric began to droop by the end of the day. However, in 1564, Mistress Dinghen van der Plasse taught Londoners to use starch to keep ruffs stiff all day. She later opened up a successful starching business.

Female Fashion

Women's dresses often mimicked the lavish gowns worn by Queen Elizabeth I. Similar to men, women wore large ruffs around their necks. They also wore farthingales, which were **petticoats** worn around the waist that flared skirts out around the body. The wide skirts contrasted with tight **corsets**, which left women looking as though they had long, skinny torsos, short legs, and wide bottoms. Women often dyed their hair or wore elaborate wigs adorned with jewels. They completed their looks by wearing white face makeup and staining their lips and cheeks bright shades of red.

Toxic Beauty

Pale, white skin was fashionable and a sign of wealth or noble status. This is because the light-skinned nobility had the luxury of remaining indoors instead of working outside where they would tan. For others, the look was achieved through white face makeup; unknown to them, the makeup was a poisonous mixture of powdered bones, lead, and vinegar.

Inside the Home

Life for English citizens differed based on social class, and housing was no exception. Houses varied greatly throughout England. Nobility lived in large stone homes with many rooms and large outdoor gardens. They emphasized luxury with gold walls and fancy materials. Merchants typically lived in wooden or stone homes above their stores. However, the majority of Londoners were poor and lived in very small homes. The floors were made of dirt, and the ceilings were poor constructions made of sticks, mud, and plants, or **thatch**.

Fireplaces blazed with fires to keep the rooms warm and to provide much-needed light. Candles were used instead of lamps. Eventually, as glass became more affordable, windows became larger, allowing for more natural light.

Most homes had at least one dining chamber and one bedroom. The larger homes had more rooms, including kitchens, offices, closets, halls for social gatherings, servants' quarters, and maybe even music rooms. After long days, people would retire to their bedrooms. However, beds were often nothing more than straw pallets on the floor with thin blankets for covering. To own a bed with a feather mattress was a real extravagance!

Home Sweet Home

In 1597, Shakespeare bought a home in Stratford. It was the second largest home in town. He called it New Place, and it was very luxurious, with 20 rooms, 10 fireplaces, and an impressive garden. Shakespeare paid nearly $100 for his home, which is equivalent to about $2.7 million today.

Laundry Day

People hand-washed their clothing and hung it to dry. Instead of soap, many people made use of the sterile and cleansing power of ammonia. This was found in urine! Special containers were used to collect urine, and it was used to treat tough stains on fabric.

What to Eat

Just like today, mealtimes were important social gatherings in Shakespeare's world. An English person's home typically had one dining chamber with a large table surrounded by small stools. Normally, the host of the household sat at the head of the table. Family and friends came together, shared meals, and updated each other on the latest gossip or theater productions.

People usually consumed three meals per day. Breakfast was eaten early in the morning before heading to work. Dinner was eaten in the midafternoon. The final meal of the day was supper.

The lower classes fit meals around their work schedules. Merchants would close their shops and sit down to meals with their friends and families. The nobility had the freedom and flexibility in their schedules to eat whenever they pleased. The wealthy citizens usually had large feasts for supper, followed by plenty of dancing, music, and entertainment. Excessive amounts of food were prepared for these large feasts, and the leftovers were often given to the servants and the poor.

Don't Forget Your Spoon!

If invited to supper at someone's house, you would be expected to bring your own utensils. Guests arrived with their knives and spoons in their pockets or attached to their belts. (Most people did not eat with forks at this time.) Those who could afford them would carry utensils in fancy boxes.

Spice It Up

English food was heavily spiced during this time period. People sought out spices from the Far East. Meats were coated in pepper, honey, cinnamon, and cloves.

The diets of people in Elizabethan England were varied and nutritious. Bread was part of every meal, and just like today, eggs were often eaten for breakfast. Stews and porridges were common meals enjoyed by all social classes. People believed that raw foods were unhealthy, so vegetables and fruits were always cooked. Meat was only consumed by those who could afford it, and typical meats were beef, pork, chicken, and rabbit. The law required all people to eat fish instead of meat on certain days of the week to support the fishing industry. Meals usually ended with desserts of fruit pies and tarts.

Fast Food

Even during Shakespeare's time, there was a demand for food that could be eaten on the go. When people attended the theater, there were food booths where they could purchase biscuits with cheese, skewers of meat, or sweet pies and pastries for dessert.

An interesting aspect of the English diet during this time was the choice of beverages. Few people chose to drink water, fearing that it was contaminated and carried disease. And of course, there were no cans of soda, juice boxes, or bottles of water for sale! So everyone, including children, drank beer, ale, cider, and wine.

Wisely, people understood that food played a role in one's health and well-being. Most medicines were made from plants and herbs and helped with illnesses such as headaches and stomach pain. Cookbooks typically contained recipes for medicines as well as meals.

Baked Goods

Some homes did not have ovens, so women waited for the baker's apprentice to come around town. He let them know when they could send their homemade pies or cakes to the bakehouse to be baked that day.

Health and Hygiene

Antibacterial soap, toothpaste, deodorant, and toilets—sadly, none of these things existed in Elizabethan England. In London, there was no indoor plumbing. People went to the bathroom in chamber pots, which were then dumped onto the city streets. Imagine the germs, horrid smells, and disgusting sludge that filled the cramped city!

Despite the filthy living conditions, many residents of the dirty city practiced simple hygiene. They used their fingers or small pieces of cloth to "brush" their teeth. Some people used small pieces of wood as toothpicks to dislodge food stuck in their teeth. Most people washed their faces and hands with rags and water on a daily basis.

Why Not a Bath?

Baths were not practical in Tudor England. It was too difficult to bring enough clean water to one's home in buckets, let alone warm it over the fire. Plus, common people did not have bathtubs—those were typically for royalty only.

Because of the dirty and crowded living conditions, diseases ran **rampant** in the city. If the death toll reached a certain number, an **epidemic** was declared. One of the worst epidemics repeatedly to strike Elizabethan England was the bubonic plague. If the plague hit your home, a cross would be painted on the door, and your home would be nailed shut so no one could go in or out.

That Smells Lovely

For those who could afford them, there were scented soaps and perfumes. However, these were considered luxury items that were used to show off how rich people were. They were only used to hide or mask the smells associated with improper hygiene.

Players and Playhouses

Talented playwrights, such as Shakespeare and Christopher Marlowe, drew large crowds to theaters. At first, plays in Elizabethan England were performed on traveling carts, in the courtyards of local inns, or on royal grounds. They were moving productions that did not stay in one location for very long. However, after 1575, permanent theaters were built just outside of London. The first two were called The Theatre and The Curtain.

Actors, called players, would bring playwrights' words to life. Being an actor was a new, risky profession. Players were considered wild and disruptive and were not held in high regard. Players were part of troupes, and they were all men. It was illegal for women to perform in public settings because it was considered inappropriate. Young boys typically played female roles.

Many players had more than one part in their plays, and some would be in more than one play at a time; thus, they had to memorize many, many lines. Players had to know how to sing and dance, and they needed to have sword-fighting skills. Playhouses had no lights to illuminate the stages, so players would **rehearse** in the mornings and perform in the afternoons.

Touring Companies
When outbreaks of the plague closed theaters, acting troupes would often go on tour and perform around the country.

Move Over, Boys!

In 1629, a French acting troupe of men *and* women came to perform in England. The women were booed off the stage! It wasn't until 30 years later that a female actress played Desdemona in Shakespeare's *Othello*. This marked a turning point for female actors in English theater.

Shakespearean Theaters

There were two types of theaters during Shakespeare's time: outdoor or public and indoor or private. Outdoor theaters were more popular since they held more people and were affordable. These theaters varied in size and shape but had some similar features.

1. **Trapdoor and cellar**—allowed actors to magically appear on stage from underneath

2. **Props**—served as clues for the audience
   - example—candles indicated nightime

3. **Balconies**—represented high windows or castle ledges; highest balcony held musicians or royalty

4. **Pillars**—supported the roof; typically painted with stars to look like the heavens

5. **Upper rooms**—held items that produced sound effects

6. **Flags**—indicated the genre of play being performed
   - black—tragedy
   - white—comedy
   - red—history

7. **Seating**—based on wealth

8. **Yard**—standing-room-only viewing area without a roof; entrance cost one penny

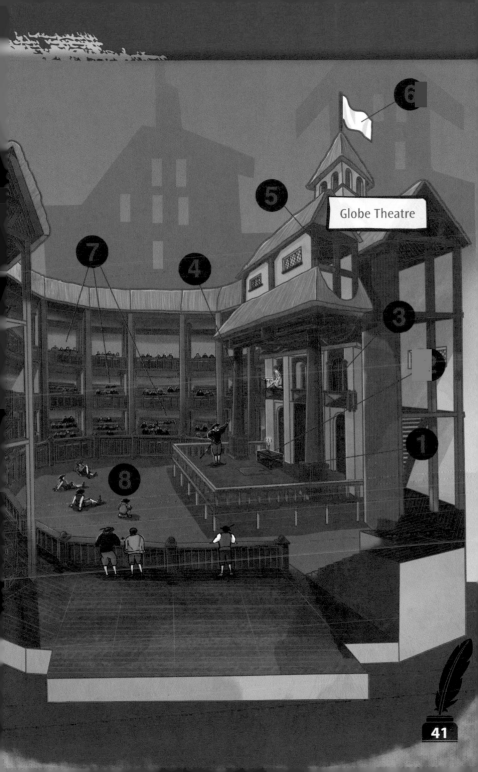

Globe Theatre

All the World's a Stage

Audiences flocked to theaters to see Shakespeare's plays because they were different from other plays at that time. Some told stories about the history of England, which was a bold and new technique. Other plays were about faraway lands. Furthermore, Shakespeare's characters were complex. He wrote his heroes with flaws, making them more human and relatable. He wrote his villains in ways that audiences would feel sorrow for them no matter how immoral or corrupt they were. And Shakespeare was known for his humor. His plays had funny **quips** and insults that made audiences roar with laughter.

Living in London during the Tudor period was exciting and vibrant. Shakespeare met many different kinds of people and lived through such historical events as the defeat of the Spanish Armada and outbreaks of the plague. People, places, and events all shaped and inspired Shakespeare's words and works. His world was the backdrop for his universally appealing and immortal plays. As Shakespeare wrote, "All the world's a stage," and his writing undoubtedly proved it so.

The Spanish Armada

In 1588, 130 Spanish ships known as the Armada approached the southern coast of England to gain control of the English Channel. But the English were ready. They used long-range guns to blast the Spanish ships. After several days, the Spanish fleet was forced back out to sea.

Is Shakespeare Shakespeare?

Some experts question the identity of William Shakespeare. They think it is far-fetched that a middle-class man from a small town would possess the skills, experience, and knowledge to write the works attributed to him. Some theories claim that famous playwright Christopher Marlowe wrote the plays, while others say the seventeenth Earl of Oxford, Edward de Vere, wrote them. Are the theories real or "much ado about nothing"? We may never know.

Edward de Vere

Christopher Marlowe

Glossary

allusions—references to things without mentioning them directly

baptized—gave a child a name and made pure in spirit; typically involves the sprinkling of water on the head

censor—to examine things in order to remove objectionable content

corsets—tight, stiff articles of clothing worn mainly by women under clothes to make their waists appear smaller

disbanded—broke up, as in a band or a theater group

epidemic—the widespread outbreak of a disease in a region

gentry—wealthy members of society who can bear coats of arms but are not of noble rank

illiterate—unable to read or write

lymph nodes—part of the lymphatic system that fights off diseases

mandatory—required by law or rules

monarch—king or queen

morals—people's beliefs as to what is right or wrong

ordained—officially named someone to rule

patron—person who gives money, goods, and support to an artist or an organization

persecution—treating people unfairly or cruelly because of their religious beliefs

petticoats—full and often ruffled skirts worn under dresses

plague—disease that is caused by bacteria and results in a high rate of death

pomanders—clove-studded oranges or apples carried to avoid catching the plague

psychology—the study of the human mind and behavior

quills—pens made from the hollow parts of feathers

quips—clever or funny remarks or sayings

rampant—spreading very quickly in a way that is difficult to control

rehearse—to practice and prepare for a public performance

sonnets—poems made up of 14 lines with fixed rhyme patterns

squires—young men who aided knights before becoming knights themselves

thatch—roofing made of dried plant materials

troupes—companies or groups of actors who perform together

yeomanry—the middle class, typically made up of landowners who were skilled in a craft or trade; a class of people below the gentry

Index

Check It Out!

This is an abbreviated list of William Shakespeare's titles and original printing dates you might be interested in checking out!

Comedy of Errors, The (1594)
Julius Caesar (1599)
King Lear (1605)
Macbeth (1606)
Midsummer Night's Dream, A (1595)
Much Ado About Nothing (1598)
Romeo and Juliet (1594)

Books

Carbone, Courtney. 2015. *srsly Hamlet*. Random House Books for Young Readers.

Chrisp, Peter. 2015. *Eyewitness: Shakespeare*. DK.

Cooney, Caroline B. 2008. *Enter Three Witches*. Scholastic Paperbacks.

Roberts, Russell. 2010. *How'd They Do That in Elizabethan England?* Mitchell Lane.

Shakespeare, William. 2005. *The Oxford Shakespeare: The Complete Works 2nd Edition*. Oxford University Press.

Shuter, Paul. 2014. *William Shakespeare: A Man for All Times*. Heisman Library.